BASIC & PASCAL

by
S. J. WAINWRIGHT
B.Sc., Ph.D., M.I.Biol.

**BERNARD BABANI (publishing) LTD
THE GRAMPIANS
SHEPHERDS BUSH ROAD
LONDON W6 7NF
ENGLAND**

Although every care has been taken with the preparation of this book, the publishers or author will not be held responsible in any way for any errors that might occur.

© 1983 BERNARD BABANI (publishing) LTD

First Published — May 1983

British Library Cataloguing in Publication Data
Wainwright, S. J.
 Basic & Pascal in parallel.
 1. BASIC (computer program language)
 2. Pascal (computer program language)
 I. Title
 001.64'24   QA76.3.B3

ISBN 0 85934 101 1

Printed and bound in Great Britain by Cox & Wyman Ltd, Reading

CONTENTS

Page

INTRODUCTION 1

GOOD PROGRAMMING 3
   What is a good program? 3

THE DEVELOPMENT OF A COMPUTER PROGRAM 3
   Stage 1 Defining the jobs required of the program 3
   Stage 2 Devising the program 4
   Stage 3 Coding the program 4
   Stage 4 Testing and debugging 4
   Stage 5 Use of the program 4
   Stage 6 Maintenance 5
   The appendages to a good program 5
   The structure of a good program 5
   The flow of control 6

PROGRAM BUILDING 6
   Output to the screen 6
   Printing numbers on the screen 9

ARITHMETIC 11
   Arithmetic operators 11
   Real number arithmetic operators 12
   Integer arithmetic operators 12
   Assignment of values to variables 13
   A short arithmetic program 13
   Standard library Functions 15
   User defined Functions 16
   Local variables and Global variables 19

PASCAL PROCEDURES AND BASIC SUBROUTINES . . . 21
   Passing Parameters to Procedures 26
   Calling Procedures and subroutines more than once 27
   Relational operators 29

	Page
Boolean expressions	30
Boolean operators	30
CONTROL STRUCTURES	**30**
Conditional branches	30
Repetition and FOR loops	32
REPEAT UNTIL loops	35
WHILE loops	37
ARRAYS	**39**
DATA, READ and RESTORE statements	42
RECURSION	**44**
Structured sorting programs	46
APPENDIX 1: Standard PASCAL	**58**
PROGRAM	58
Writing strings	59
Comments	59
ARRAY declaration	59
TYPE declaration	60
APPENDIX 2: Creating 2 or 3 dimensional ARRAYS from a 1 dimensional ARRAY	**60**

INTRODUCTION

BASIC was developed at Dartmouth College in the mid 1960's by John Kemeny and Thomas Kurtz. The word BASIC stands for Beginners All purpose Symbolic Instruction Code.

PASCAL was developed by Niklaus Wirth in Zurich in 1971. PASCAL is named in honour of the French mathematician Blaise Pascal who developed one of the first mechanical calculators in the seventeenth century.

BASIC is said to be the simplest of the high level computer languages to learn. It was developed as a language which would be simple to learn and use, and would thus provide a suitable introduction to high level computer programming. However, whilst BASIC is undoubtedly the easiest language in which to code programs, it is arguable as to whether it is in fact a suitable language in which to start learning programming. This is because most versions of BASIC which are available on mainframe and microcomputers are not structured. Even those versions of BASIC which contain many of the features of structured languages do not *force* structure on the programs written. This is not to say that structured programming cannot be carried out in BASIC because this is not so, as will be seen throughout this text. However, the structure present in any program in BASIC is imposed by the programmer *not* by the language itself. It is therefore clear that if a person begins by coding programs in BASIC which are unstructured, he/she will develop an unstructured way of thinking about programming which will be unusable in languages such as Algol or PASCAL. Consequently, a writer of unstructured BASIC programs will have difficulty in moving over into a language such as PASCAL which demands a structured approach. Conversely, a writer of structured BASIC programs will have little difficulty in switching over to PASCAL when the need arises.

PASCAL was developed essentially as a language with which to teach programming because it forces structure into the program as it is written. However, PASCAL has been widely adopted as a language suitable for real applications rather than simply as a teaching language. Moreover, whereas

BASIC is a very friendly language in which it is easy to make programs work, PASCAL is rather less friendly to the newcomer, and it makes more demands on the programmer to design his/her program *before* coding begins.

This text will take the two languages BASIC and PASCAL, and will develop the idea of programming in both languages simultaneously. This will be done by using BASIC to emulate PASCAL wherever possible. In this way we shall impose PASCAL-like structure on our BASIC programs. As a consequence of following this approach, the techniques of good programming, which are imposed by PASCAL will become embedded in the way we think about BASIC programs. The BASIC will remain as friendly as ever, and as we shall in many cases be virtually writing PASCAL programs in BASIC, the PASCAL itself should appear just as friendly.

BASIC and PASCAL are both available as compiled or interpreted implementations on various systems. BASIC is usually interpreted, and PASCAL is usually compiled. However, the BASIC and the PASCAL used to develop the programs given in this text are both interpreted versions. A Sharp MZ80 microcomputer was used, and the programs given here will run under the SP5025 BASIC and the SP4015 PASCAL interpreters (unless indicated by ***). As these are very standard implementations of the two languages, the reader should have little difficulty in using other interpreters or compilers. Appendix 1. shows the major differences between SP4015 PASCAL and Standard PASCAL.

This text is not intended to cover in depth *all* of the features of both languages, but rather, to develop a way of thinking about BASIC and PASCAL programming which is compatible with both languages, and to practice the building of programs in both languages.

This text could be used as an introduction to programming in either BASIC or PASCAL. It could be used by an experienced BASIC programmer who wishes to learn PASCAL, or it could help a BASIC programmer to rethink his/her approach to BASIC programming. Finally, as the title suggests, it could be used to learn *both* BASIC and PASCAL *at the same time*. It is intended for all of these uses.

GOOD PROGRAMMING

With BASIC it is possible to sit down at the computer and compose programs at the keyboard.

With PASCAL this is impossible with all but the most trivial of programs. In PASCAL a program has to be designed *before* it is written, whereas in BASIC, a freestyle approach of designing the program as you go along can achieve *workable* results.

Most people begin by programming in BASIC in this freestyle way, and it is at this early stage that programming habits are developed which are incompatible with those demanded by a language such as PASCAL. Moreover, they are incompatible with concepts of good programming, and with concepts of collaboration in program writing with other programmers.

What is a good program?

It is not sufficient for a program to work, it must *always* work. It must not only be seen to work, it must also be seen *how* it works. It must not only perform a given set of operations, it must be capable from time to time, of having modifications made, and some of these operations changed easily.

In order to achieve these ends, the *modular* approach of structured programming should be used. PASCAL imposes a certain amount of structure on a program, but a BASIC programmer can impose similar structure on his/her BASIC programs.

THE DEVELOPMENT OF A COMPUTER PROGRAM

Stage 1 Defining the jobs required of the program

This stage is carried out by a person with a vested interest in the program. He/she may be the end user, or he may be a project director etc. This person need never be personally involved with the use of a computer.

Stage 2 Devising the program

The details of exactly how the various jobs of the program are going to be done, and in what order they are to be done, are worked out and written down either as lists, flowcharts or Nassi Shneider diagrams. This is the *actual* programming stage. The formal writing down of the program is in many ways independent of the computer language to be used. This stage is carried out by the programmer.

Stage 3 Coding the program

When the appropriate language for the job has been selected, the program is then coded into BASIC or PASCAL etc. according to the structure devised in stage 2. This stage is carried out by the programmer, or possibly by several programmers, each coding a different part of the program. Notice that we have drawn a distinction between programming and coding. A program once written can possibly be coded into several languages. A common mistake (in terms of the development of bad programming habits) made by BASIC programmers, is to combine stages 2 and 3.

Stage 4 Testing and debugging

Once a program has been coded into BASIC or PASCAL it is *then* typed into the computer, and run with various sets of data for which the results are known, and which cover a realistic range of likely values. Errors and bugs are removed and the program is stored for future use, possibly on magnetic tape or disc. This stage is carried out by the programmer, possibly in collaboration with the end user.

Stage 5 Use of the Program

The program is used for its intended applications by the end user.

Stage 6 Maintenance

From time to time modifications may be required to be made to the program. For example in a very simple case, a business program which incorporates a V.A.T. tax calculation would have to be changed if the government changed the V.A.T. rate. This stage would be carried out by a programmer who may not have been involved with the original writing of the program. This is why one of the criteria of a good program is that it should be possible to see easily exactly how the program works.

The appendages to a good program

To facilitate the understanding and maintenance of a program, it should have a modular structure, and should be accompanied by adequate documentation. The documentation should explain what the various parts of the program do, and how to operate the program. The documentation can be both internal and external to the program.

Internal documentation takes the form of comment or remark statements within the program which are ignored by the interpreter or compiler. The function of the comment or remark statements is to provide information within the program listing which will assist in the understanding of the program, and hence in its maintenance.

External documentation consists of notes which describe the structure, function and operation of the program.

The structure of a good program

A good program should consist of a series of sub-programs, each of which performs a particular function; and a main program whose job it is to call the various sub-programs in the correct order. With this kind of program structure, it is the sub-programs which do most of the work. The main program just specifies which sub-program will be working at any particular time.

The flow of control

A computer program consists of a sequence of instructions which are carried out in order by the machine. The instructions to be carried out are called statements. In order that they can be carried out in sequence, the statements have to be separated from each other. In PASCAL, a semi-colon serves as a separator between statements, and a space serves as a separator between words within a statement. In BASIC, statement separation can be achieved by typing each statement with a different line number. Some versions of BASIC allow statement separation to be achieved within a line by means of a colon. In most versions of BASIC, no spaces are needed to separate words within a statement.

In this text we shall follow the rule of one statement per line, but the semi-colon will still be necessary in PASCAL.

During the execution of a program, control passes from one statement to the next, in the sequence indicated by the program.

PROGRAM BUILDING

Output to the screen

The simplest program which we can imagine is one to cause the computer to print out a single character on the display screen.

In PASCAL we begin with the word BEGIN and we finish with the word END.

PASCAL
Program 1

```
BEGIN
   WRITE("A")
END.
```

Note the full stop after the word END at the end of the program.

In BASIC BEGIN does not exist, and END is not usually needed. However, we shall include END in our programs to emphasise the similarity between the PASCAL and the BASIC programs, and also because in some implementations of BASIC, END is actually required.

BASIC
Program 2

```
100 PRINT"A"
110 END
```

We shall start as we mean to go on, and will include internal documentation in the form of comments or remarks.

In PASCAL, comments are enclosed within two % signs. In BASIC, remarks are preceded by the word REM. Comments and remarks are ignored by the interpreter or compiler and are present only as internal documentation.

PASCAL

```
%PROGRAM 3%
%THIS PRINTS A SINGLE CHARACTER%
BEGIN
   WRITE("A")
END.
```

BASIC

```
100 REM PROGRAM 4
110 REM THIS PRINTS A SINGLE CHARACTER
120 PRINT"A"
130 END
```

PASCAL has another printing command WRITELN which means WRITE and then move to a new line. Consider the difference in effect between the following PASCAL and BASIC programs:

PASCAL

```
%PROGRAM 5%
%THIS PRINTS TWO CHARACTERS%
BEGIN
   WRITE("A");
   WRITE("B")
END.
```

Note the use of the semi-colon separator.

BASIC

```
100 REM PROGRAM 6
110 REM THIS PRINTS TWO CHARACTERS
120 PRINT"A"
130 PRINT"B"
140 END
```

The PASCAL machine will print out:

    AB

whereas the BASIC machine will print out:

    A
    B

To obtain the same effect as BASIC, we have to use WRITELN instead of WRITE as follows:

PASCAL

```
%PROGRAM 7%
%THIS PRINTS TWO CHARACTERS%
BEGIN
   WRITELN("A");
   WRITELN("B")
END.
```

It is possible to print out a *string* of characters in exactly the same way that we printed a single character:

> WRITE("string")   or
> WRITELN("string")   in PASCAL and:
> PRINT"string"   in BASIC.

Printing numbers on the screen

We shall consider a short program to input a real number from the keyboard, and to print it out on the screen. In PASCAL we have to *declare* a variable before it is used because PASCAL distinguishes between real numbers and integers. The declaration of a variable is achieved by means of VAR and a colon :

PASCAL

```
%PROGRAM 8%
%INPUT AND OUTPUT OF A NUMBER%
VAR
  V:REAL;
BEGIN
  READLN(V);
  WRITELN(V)
END.
```

The command READLN or READ can be used to input a number from the keyboard. If READ is used, the number V would be printed out on the same line that it was input in program 8. If READLN is used, the number V would be printed out on the next line. The reader should try the program using READ and READLN.

BASIC

```
100 REM PROGRAM 9
110 REM INPUT AND OUTPUT OF A NUMBER
120 INPUTV
130 PRINTV
140 END
```

In BASIC it is not necessary to declare that the variable V is a real number because it treats all numbers as reals. (Some implementations of BASIC allow the declaration of integer variables.)

Within a WRITELN statement in PASCAL, or a PRINT statement in BASIC it is possible to output the value of an expression if required.

In the PASCAL program, substitute the line:

WRITELN(V*1.5)

In the BASIC program, substitute the line:

130 PRINTV*1.5

In both cases, the value that is output to the screen will be 1.5 times the input value.

PASCAL however, allows greater control over the format of the output number than does BASIC. This is because it is possible to specify within a WRITE or WRITELN statement, either one or two *fieldwidth parameters*.

For example, the statement:

WRITELN(V:10:2)

contains the two fieldwidth parameters, 10 and 2 respectively. These parameters control the printout so that the value of V is printed out at the right hand end of a field of 10 printing positions, and that it is printed out to 2 decimal places. In order to illustrate this, the symbol — will be used to denote a blank space. Thus, if V has a value of 3.426, it will be printed out as:

Fieldwidth of 10

------3.42

2 decimal places

It is possible to omit the second fieldwidth parameter, and thus print out a number to all of its decimal places but within a specified fieldwidth, e.g.:

WRITELN(V:10)

will produce the print out:

-----3.426

With the SP4015 PASCAL interpreter used here, the field-width default value is 15. This means that if no fieldwidth parameters are specified, the machine will provide a fieldwidth of 15. Different machines will have different fieldwidth default values.

In BASIC, the TAB statement gives a different kind of control over printing positions. For example:

130PRINTTAB(10);V

will *start* to print V ten printing positions from the left of the screen.

ARITHMETIC

Arithmetic operators

In BASIC the arithmetic operators are:

- \+ addition
- − subtraction
- * multiplication
- / division
- ↑ exponentiation (sometimes ** is used instead of ↑).

The order of execution of the arithmetic operations in the evaluation of expressions follows a fixed hierarchy which can be overridden by the use of parentheses.

Exponentiation has the highest priority.

Multiplication and division have equal priority which is below the priority of exponentiation but above addition and subtraction, which also have equal priority.

In PASCAL there are a set of arithmetic operators for integer arithmetic, and a set for real number arithmetic. The two kinds of number cannot be mixed directly in a single expression. There is no operator for exponentiation in PASCAL.

Real number arithmetic operators

+ addition
− subtraction
* multiplication
/ division

Integer arithmetic operators

+ addition
− subtraction
* multiplication
DIV gives the quotient of a division
MOD gives the remainder of a division

Whilst most versions of BASIC do not support the operators DIV and MOD because they do not generally support true integer arithmetic, it is possible to achieve the same results in BASIC as follows:

PASCAL	BASIC
X MOD Y	X−(Y*INT(X/Y))
X DIV Y	INT(X/Y)

The meaning of INT in BASIC will be explained below.

As it is not possible in PASCAL to evaluate arithmetic expressions which contain both real and integer variables, PASCAL provides ways of converting real numbers to integers, and integers to real numbers.

FLOAT(V) converts an integer V to a real number.

TRUNC(V) converts a real number V to an integer by truncating at the decimal point. Thus TRUNC(5.75) returns a value of 5.

In BASIC, INT(V) converts a real number V to an integer rather like the TRUNC(V) in PASCAL. However, the integer thus produced is still treated as a real number by the interpreter.

Assignment of values to variables

In PASCAL this is achieved by means of a colon followed by an equals sign. For example:

> C:= 2.5*V

assigns the value of 2.5 times the value of the variable V to the variable C. (C and V would both be real variables here). This is read as "C becomes equal to 2.5 times the value of V".

In BASIC this is achieved by the use of an equals sign alone. For example:

> 100 C=2.5*V

means "C becomes equal to 2.5 times the value of V".

Some versions of BASIC require LET before the C in the above expression. Other versions of BASIC allow the use of LET but do not require it. For example:

> 100LETC=2.5*V

A short arithmetic program

This program will input two real numbers, multiply them together, and print out the product on the screen.

PASCAL

```
%PROGRAM 10%
%PRODUCT OF TWO NUMBERS%
VAR
  A,B,C:REAL;
BEGIN
  READLN(A);
  READLN(B);
  C:=A*B;
  WRITELN("THE PRODUCT IS",C)
END.
```

BASIC

```
100 REM PROGRAM 11
110 REM PRODUCT OF TWO NUMBERS
120 INPUTA
130 INPUTB
140 C=A*B
150 PRINT"THE PRODUCT IS ";C
160 END
```

The reader should practice these programs using other arithmetic operators instead of *. The following programs perform integer divisions to obtain the quotient and the remainder.

PASCAL

```
%PROGRAM 12%
%INTEGER ARITHMETIC%
VAR
  A,B,C,D:INTEGER;
BEGIN
  WRITELN("INPUT A AND B");
  READLN(A,B);
  C:=A DIV B;
  D:=A MOD B;
  WRITELN("QUOTIENT=",C);
  WRITELN("REMAINDER=",D)
END.
```

BASIC

```
100 REM PROGRAM 13
110 REM INTEGER ARITHMETIC SIMULATION
120 PRINT"INPUT A AND B"
130 INPUTA,B
140 C=INT(A/B)
150 D=A-(B*C)
160 PRINT"QUOTIENT= ";C
170 PRINT"REMAINDER= ";D
```

180 END

So we can see that even though most versions of BASIC do not support the integer operators DIV and MOD, it is possible to achieve the same effect by another route.

Standard library Functions

We have already come across some standard library Functions in the form of FLOAT and TRUNC in PASCAL, and INT in BASIC.

A standard library Function performs a prescribed task on a specified *parameter* which is enclosed in brackets. For example, in BASIC the INT Function, which is written in the form: INT(V) where V is called the *formal parameter* of the Function. A value assigned to V is called an *actual* parameter.

For example:

        INT(4.56) returns a value of 4 whilst
        INT(−4.56) returns a value of −5. However,
in PASCAL
        TRUNC(4.56) returns a value of 4 whilst
        TRUNC(−4.56) returns a value of −4.

        ABS(V) occurs in both PASCAL and BASIC, and returns the absolute value of V.

        SQR(V) in BASIC, and
        SQRT(V) in PASCAL return the square root of V.
        EXP(V) occurs in both PASCAL and BASIC, and returns the value of e^V, where e=2.7182818.

There are standard library Functions for computing logarithms, and they vary from system to system. In both SP5025 BASIC and SP4015 PASCAL used here:

        LN(V) returns $\log_e V$ and
        LOG(V) returns $\log_{10} V$.

In some implementations only natural logarithms are available as a standard library Function.

RND(V) occurs in both BASIC and PASCAL, and returns a pseudo random number in the interval 0.00000001 to 0.99999999. The value of V affects the calculation of the pseudo random number, and reference should be made to manual for the implementation being used. Frequently, V should be a positive real number in order to obtain a sequence of pseudo random numbers.

SIN(V) is available in both PASCAL and BASIC, and returns the sine of V; which must be expressed in radians, and must be a real number for PASCAL.

TAN(V) is common to both languages and returns the tangent of V; which must be expressed in radians, and must be a real number for PASCAL.

> ATN(V) in BASIC and
> ARCTAN(V) in PASCAL return $\tan^{-1} V$.

The parameter V must be a real number in the range $-\pi/2$ to $+\pi/2$, and must be expressed in radians.

FLOAT(V) occurs in PASCAL as we have seen, and returns the floating point equivalent of the integer V.

There may be other standard library Functions available in various implementations of PASCAL or BASIC, and these should be studied for the implementation which is available to the reader.

User defined Functions

The standard library Functions provide most of the common Functions required by programmers. However, it is frequently the case that a required Function is not present in the standard library of the language. When this happens it is possible to declare a *User defined Function* to suit your own particular needs. In both PASCAL and BASIC, the Function must be declared in the program before it can be used. For example, suppose we wish to have available a Function which will return the inverse of a number. This could be achieved as follows:

PASCAL

```
%PROGRAM 14%
%INVERSE OF A NUMBER%
VAR
  V,C:REAL;
FUNCTION INV(X:REAL):REAL;
  BEGIN
    INV:=1.0/X
  END;
BEGIN %MAIN PROGRAM%
  WRITELN("INPUT A VALUE");
  READLN(V);
  C:=INV(V);
  WRITELN("INVERSE=",C)
END.
```

The first part of this program declares the variables V and C to be real numbers. The next part of the program declares the Function INV to have a parameter X which is real, and to produce a real result. The Function INV is then defined as calculating the inverse of the parameter X. Then comes the main program as indicated by the comment between the %% symbols. It is the job of the main program in this case, to prompt the user to input a value, to then receive the value V from the keyboard, and to call the User defined Function, passing the value V to its parameter X, and to assign the result of the Function to the variable C. Finally, the main program outputs the value of C with a message that it is the inverse.

A point to note is that the computational work of this program was not performed by the main program itself, but by a kind of sub-program, the User defined Function, which was called by the main program.

We can see that our programs are beginning to take on *structure* in the form of parts which perform specific tasks (such as the User defined Function INV in this case), and the main program which specifies the order in which the tasks are to be carried out. Following is the same program in BASIC.

BASIC

```
100 REM PROGRAM 15
110 REM INVERSE OF A NUMBER
120 DEF FNI(X)=1/X
130 REM MAIN PROGRAM
140    PRINT"INPUT A VALUE"
150    INPUTV
160    C=FNI(V)
170    PRINT"INVERSE= ";C
180 END
```

This program has the same structure as the PASCAL version. The declaration of the User defined Function is done on line 120 by means of the DEF FN statement. The Function is named FN I and has the parameter X.

The job of a Function, whether a standard library Function, or a User defined Function, is always to return a single value as its result. Most versions of BASIC only allow a User defined Function to have a single parameter, although some versions do allow more than one. In PASCAL, more than one parameter are allowed in User defined Functions. A short example below computes the perimeter of a rectangle given the length and width.

PASCAL

```
%PROGRAM 16%
%PERIMETER CALCULATION%
VAR
  L,W,P:REAL;
FUNCTION PERIM(LENGTH,WIDTH:REAL):REAL;
  BEGIN
     PERIM:=2.0*(LENGTH+WIDTH)
  END;
BEGIN %MAIN PROGRAM%
  WRITELN("INPUT LENGTH AND WIDTH");
  READLN(L,W);
```

```
      P:=PERIM(L,W);
      WRITELN("PERIMETER=",P)
   END.
```

In this case the Function PERIM has two parameters, length and width. For an exercise, write down the BASIC equivalent of this program assuming that you can define a Function with two parameters : DEF FNP(L,W)= which is the way to declare the Function. If your version of BASIC allows the definition of Functions with more than one parameter, then try it out on your own machine.

Local variables and Global variables

In PASCAL it is possible to declare variables within a User defined Function. We can see how this is done by modifying program 14 to produce program 17 below.

It can be seen that we have declared two variables called V. The first V is declared at the beginning of the program. This is a Global variable, i.e. it is valid throughout the program. The second V is declared inside the declaration of the User defined Function INV. This is a Local variable i.e. it is valid only within the User defined Function. In other words, whatever happens to the value of V within the User defined Function, the value of V within the main program remains unchanged. This point is illustrated in program 17 by including the line:

WRITELN("ORIGINAL=",V)

PASCAL

```
%PROGRAM 17%
%INVERSE AND ORIGINAL NUMBER%
VAR
   V,C:REAL;
FUNCTION INV(X:REAL):REAL;
   VAR
      V:REAL;
   BEGIN
```

```
      V:=1.0/X;
      INV:=V
   END;
BEGIN %MAIN PROGRAM%
   WRITELN("INPUT A VALUE");
   READLN(V);
   C:=INV(V);
   WRITELN("INVERSE=",C);
   WRITELN("ORIGINAL=",V)
END.
```

Suppose when we run the program, we input the number 5.0 in the line:

        READLN(V);

So the global variable V takes the value 5.0

The next line:

        C:= INV(V);

then passes 5.0 as the parameter X to the Function INV. Then, within the Function INV, the local variable V is assigned the value of 1.0/5.0 i.e. 0.2 in the line:

        V:= 1.0/X;

The line:

        WRITELN("ORIGINAL=",V)

confirms that despite the fact that the local variable V has taken the value of 0.2 in the User defined Function INV, the global variable V has retained its original value of 5.0.

If we do not declare V as a local variable within the User defined Function, the V within that Function refers to the global variable V, which will consequently be changed by the line:

        V:= 1.0/X;

Once again, this is confirmed by the line:

WRITELN("ORIGINAL=",V)

This is illustrated by program 18 below.

PASCAL

```
%PROGRAM 18%
%INVERSE AND ORIGINAL CHANGED%
VAR
   V,C:REAL;
FUNCTION INV(X:REAL):REAL;
   BEGIN
      V:=1.0/X;
      INV:=V
   END;
BEGIN %MAIN PROGRAM%
   WRITELN("INPUT A VALUE");
   READLN(V);
   C:=INV(V);
   WRITELN("INVERSE=",C);
   WRITELN("ORIGINAL=",V)
END.
```

One advantage of the use of local variables is that different people can develop different parts of a program without having to worry that the names of the variables they use may be the same as the names of other variables used elsewhere in the program.

In most versions of BASIC all variables are global.

PASCAL PROCEDURES AND BASIC SUBROUTINES

We have already introduced the idea that the majority of the work of a program is not carried out by the main program but rather by special sub-programs such as User defined Functions or even library Functions. It is the job of the main program to call the various sub-programs in the correct order, and to pass values to the parameters of the sub-programs.

We have seen that it is possible to declare User defined Functions but that a Function can only return a single value as its result.

Frequently it is required that a sub-program should perform a large number of tasks and possibly return a large number of results. In PASCAL this can be achieved by the use of PROCEDURES, and in BASIC it can be achieved by the use of slightly different structures called SUBROUTINES. (Some versions of BASIC allow the declaration of Procedures but these are very rare.)

In order to reinforce the idea of modular programming, we shall take the modular approach to program construction to the extreme, and we shall construct sub-programs to do virtually all of the work of the program, even when it may be efficient to allow the main program to do more work. As experience is gained by the programmer, a balance can be achieved between work done by the main program, and work done by the sub-programs. However, when more than one programmer are collaborating on the writing of a program, a totally modular approach is the easiest path to follow.

The following program will input three numbers, print out their inverses, and the product and sum of the inverses. We shall use a Procedure to input the values, a Procedure to call a User defined Function to invert the values, a Procedure to compute the product and sum of the inverses, and a Procedure to print out the results. The function of the main program will simply be to call the Procedures in the correct order.

PASCAL

```
%PROGRAM 19%
%PRODUCT AND SUM OF INVERSES%
VAR
   A,B,C,P,S,I1,I2,I3:REAL;
FUNCTION INV(X:REAL):REAL;
   BEGIN
```

```
      INV:=1.0/X
   END;
PROCEDURE ENTER;
   BEGIN
      WRITELN("INPUT THREE NUMBERS");
      READLN(A,B,C)
   END;
PROCEDURE INVERT;
   BEGIN
      I1:=INV(A);
      I2:=INV(B);
      I3:=INV(C)
   END;
PROCEDURE PRODSUM;
   BEGIN
      P:=I1*I2*I3;
      S:=I1+I2+I3
   END;
PROCEDURE PRINTOUT;
   BEGIN
      WRITELN("INVERSES");
      WRITELN(I1);
      WRITELN(I2);
      WRITELN(I3);
      WRITELN("PRODUCT OF INVERSES");
      WRITELN(P);
      WRITELN("SUM OF INVERSES");
      WRITELN(S)
   END;
BEGIN %MAIN PROGRAM%
   ENTER;
   INVERT;
   PRODSUM;
   PRINTOUT
END.
```

In BASIC the subroutine can achieve the same effect as the PASCAL Procedure. In PASCAL a Procedure is called by specifying its name as shown in program 19. In BASIC a subroutine is called by a GOSUB statement. The subroutine called by the GOSUB is identified by the line number at which the subroutine starts. The end of the subroutine is marked by a RETURN statement which causes the flow of control to jump back to the line number immediately following the GOSUB which called the subroutine. Program 20 is a BASIC version of program 19.

BASIC

```
100 REM PROGRAM 20
110 REM PRODUCT AND SUM OF INVERSES
120 DEF FNI(X)=1/X
130 REM TRANSFER CONTROL TO MAIN PROG.
140 GOTO390
150 REM SUBROUTINE ENTER
160    PRINT"INPUT THREE NUMBERS"
170    INPUTA,B,C
180 RETURN
190 REM SUBROUTINE INVERT
200    I1=FNI(A)
210    I2=FNI(B)
220    I3=FNI(C)
230 RETURN
240 REM SUBROUTINE PRODSUM
250    P=I1*I2*I3
260    S=I1+I2+I3
270 RETURN
280 REM SUBROUTINE PRINTOUT
290    PRINT"INVERSES"
300    PRINTI1
310    PRINTI2
320    PRINTI3
330    PRINT"PRODUCT OF INVERSES"
```

```
340     PRINTP
350     PRINT"SUM OF INVERSES"
360     PRINTS
370 RETURN
380 REM MAIN PROGRAM
390     GOSUB160
400     GOSUB200
410     GOSUB250
420     GOSUB290
430 END
```

A difference between PASCAL Procedures and BASIC subroutines is that the flow of control passes through the Procedures as they are declared and before the main program is reached. (This is also true of User defined Functions in both BASIC and PASCAL.) However, in BASIC, the flow of control passes through subroutines only when they are called, so it is necessary to program 20 to use a GOTO statement at line 140 to divert the flow of control around the subroutines to the main program. It will also be noticed that whilst REM statements mark the start of the various subroutines and the main program, control is always passed to the line following the REM by the GOTO or the GOSUB statements. This is done for two reasons. Firstly, as a REM statement is ignored by the interpreter, there is no point in passing control to it. Secondly, if control is never passed to a REM statement, the REM can be deleted if required from the final working version of the program in order to save memory space. The REMs should however, always be retained in the printed copies of the program as they constitute the internal documentation of the program.

It will also be noticed in program 20 that we are using indenting of the listing to emphasise the structure of the program in a similar way to the indenting which is done in PASCAL. Not all BASIC interpreters will preserve indenting for purposes of listing, but when they do, indenting should be used routinely. Moreover, indenting should always be used in hand or typewritten programs.

Passing Parameters to Procedures

In program 19 when the Procedure INVERT was called by main program, this was done simply by specifying the Procedure's name INVERT at the appropriate position in the main program. It can be seen that the global variables A, B and C were passed directly into the Procedure. However, passing variables directly into the Procedure in this way severely limits the Procedure in that it can only operate on the global variables A, B and C and no others. It is possible however, to pass variables to the parameters of a Procedure and thereby give the Procedure more flexibility of use. We clearly need to pass three real numbers to the Procedure (A, B and C), and so it is necessary to declare the Procedure with three parameters. Below is the Procedure INVERT re-written in this way:

PASCAL

```
PROCEDURE INVERT(X,Y,Z:REAL):REAL;
  BEGIN
    I1:=INV(X);
    I2:=INV(Y);
    I3:=INV(Z)
  END;
```

The values A, B and C can be passed to the Procedure INVERT when it is called by the main program as follows:

```
INVERT(A,B,C);
```

These modifications should be made to program 19 and then the reader should demonstrate that the modified program gives exactly the same results as does the unmodified program.

Just as it was shown in program 17 that it is possible to declare local variables within User defined Functions, it is also possible to declare local variables within Procedures. It is possible for local variables to take the same names as global variables, and any changes which occur in the value of a local variable will not affect the value of the global variable with the same name.

Of course the parameters of a Procedure (or User defined Function) are also local variables but they have the special function of receiving values from outside the Procedure.

Calling Procedures and subroutines more than once

Procedures and subroutines come into their own when they need to be used more than once in a program because they avoid the necessity for wasteful repetition of coding. This is illustrated in programs 21 and 22. The program allows us to input two numbers and print out the inverse of each number after it is input. The PASCAL program 21 declares the global variables A and B, which are the numbers to be input. The User defined Function INV is then declared with a parameter X. The Procedure INVERT is then declared also with a parameter X (Note that the Xs are local to the Function and the Procedure respectively, so it does not matter that they have the same name.) Within the Procedure INVERT, a local variable I is declared, the User defined Function INV is called, and the result is printed out. The main program inputs a number A, and calls the Procedure INVERT, passing A as the parameter of INVERT. The Procedure does the rest. Then another number, B is input. The Procedure INVERT is called again, but this time B is passed as its parameter, and again the Procedure does the rest.

PASCAL

```
%PROGRAM 21%
%PROCEDURE CALLED TWICE%
VAR
  A,B:REAL;
FUNCTION INV(X:REAL):REAL;
  BEGIN
    INV:=1.0/X
  END;
PROCEDURE INVERT(X:REAL);
VAR
```

```
      I:REAL;
      BEGIN
        I:=INV(X);
        WRITELN("INVERSE=",I)
      END;
    BEGIN %MAIN PROGRAM%
      WRITELN("INPUT A NUMBER");
      READLN(A);
      INVERT(A);
      WRITELN("INPUT ANOTHER NUMBER");
      READLN(B);
      INVERT(B)
    END.
```

BASIC

```
100 REM PROGRAM 22
110 REM SUBROUTINE CALLED TWICE
120 DEF FNI(X)=1/X
130 REM TRANSFER CONTROL TO MAIN PROG.
140 GOTO200
150 REM SUBROUTINE INVERT
160    I=FNI(P)
170    PRINT"INVERSE= ";I
180 RETURN
190 REM MAIN PROGRAM
200    PRINT"INPUT A NUMBER"
210    INPUTA
220    P=A
230    GOSUB160
240    PRINT"INPUT ANOTHER NUMBER"
250    INPUTB
260    P=B
270    GOSUB160
280 END
```

In BASIC, User defined Functions have parameters but subroutines do not. Nevertheless, with a little extra coding, it is possible to *effectively* give parameters to a subroutine.

The BASIC program 22 declares the User defined Function FNI with a parameter X. Control is then passed to the main program by means of the GOTO statement at line 140. The main program inputs a number A at line 210. Then, before the subroutine INVERT is called, a variable P is assigned the value of A. P is a variable only used within the subroutine INVERT, and it thus behaves as a parameter of the subroutine. Then the subroutine INVERT is called at line 230. The subroutine INVERT then behaves exactly like the Procedure INVERT in the PASCAL program 21. The RETURN statement at line 180 returns control to the main program at line 240. Then another number, B is input. Again, the pseudo-parameter variable P is assigned the value of B, the subroutine INVERT is called and it does the rest.

Relational operators

Relational operators are used in conditional branch structures in conjunction with IF. They are used for comparing two data values:

   A = B checks to see whether A is equal to B

(Note that this is *not* assigning the value of B to A).

   A <> B checks whether A is not equal to B.
   A < B checks whether A is less than B.
   A > B checks whether A is greater than B.
   A <= B checks whether A is less than or equal to B.
   A >= B checks whether A is greater than or equal to B.

The result of such a comparison is always TRUE or FALSE. Thus, if A=2, and B=2 for example:

   A = B is TRUE,
   A >= B and A <= B are also TRUE.
However, A < B , A > B and A <> B are all FALSE.

Boolean expressions

A Boolean Expression produces a result of either TRUE or FALSE (NOT TRUE), and involves the use of relational operators as above, and possibly Boolean Operators as below.

Boolean operators

The Boolean operators which we shall use here are : AND and OR. The operator AND has precedence over the operator OR.

The result of a Boolean expression is always TRUE or FALSE.

Thus for example, if A=1, B=2, C=3, and D=4 :

    (A < B) AND (C < D)   is TRUE, and
    (A < B) AND (C = D)   is FALSE, moreover
    (A = B) AND (C = D)   is FALSE, however,
    (A < B) OR (C = D)   is TRUE, whilst
    (A = B) OR (C = D)   is FALSE.

In some language implementations such as the SP-5025 BASIC used here, the words AND and OR are replaced by the symbols * and + respectively. Thus, the previous expressions can be written in SP-5025 BASIC as follows:

    (A < B)*(C < D)   is TRUE, and
    (A < B)*(C = D)   is FALSE.
    (A = B)*(C = D)   is FALSE, however,
    (A < B)+(C = D)   is TRUE, whilst
    (A = B)+(C = D)   is FALSE.

We can see therefore, that (A)AND(B) is only TRUE if *both* (A) and (B) are TRUE. However, (A)OR(B) is TRUE if *either* (A) or (B) is TRUE.

CONTROL STRUCTURES

Conditional branches

Often it is required that the flow of control in a program

should be diverted down various paths depending on whether certain conditions are met or not. Consider the following program.

Input an integer. If this number is greater than ten then print out "GREATER THAN 10". Otherwise print out "NOT GREATER THAN 10".

PASCAL

```
%PROGRAM 23%
%CONDITIONAL BRANCH%
VAR
  N:INTEGER;
BEGIN
  READLN(N);
  IF N>10 THEN
  WRITELN("GREATER THAN TEN")
  ELSE
  WRITELN("NOT GREATER THAN TEN")
END.
```

Note that from IF right through to END, there are no semi-colon statement separators. This is because the IF THEN WRITELN( ) ELSE WRITELN( ) is one long statement. In PASCAL however, we can split it up into separate lines for listing, and to make the structure of the program clearer. In BASIC however, if ELSE is supported, then the IF THEN PRINT" " ELSE PRINT" " must be written as a single statement in one line, as shown by program 24 WITH ELSE.

BASIC * * *

```
100 REM PROGRAM 24 WITH ELSE
110 REM CONDITIONAL BRANCH
120 INPUTN
130 IFN>10THENPRINT"GREATER THAN TEN"
    ELSEPRINT"NOT GREATER THAN TEN"
140 END
```

However, many versions of BASIC (including the SP-5025 used here) do not support ELSE, but its effect can be easily simulated.

BASIC

```
100 REM PROGRAM 24 WITHOUT ELSE
110 REM CONDITIONAL BRANCH
120 INPUTN
130 IFN>10THEN170
140 REM SIMULATION OF ELSE
150 PRINT"NOT GREATER THAN TEN"
160 GOTO180
170 PRINT"GREATER THAN TEN"
180 END
```

In program 24 WITHOUT ELSE, the test to see whether N is greater than 10 is carried out on line 130. If the relationship is TRUE then control is transferred to line 170. If the relationship is NOT TRUE then control passes on to line 140. Line 160 is used to pass control around line 170 which is used only if the relationship is TRUE.

Repetition and FOR loops

Suppose that we wish to input several numbers and then compute their mean. This would involve repetition in that the number input stage is repeated, and the summing stage is repeated N times if N numbers are input. The repetition can be achieved by FOR loops as follows:

PASCAL

```
%PROGRAM 25%
%AVERAGE%
VAR
   I,N:INTEGER;
   A,S,M:REAL;
```

```
PROCEDURE ENTER;
  BEGIN
    S:=0.0;
    WRITELN("INPUT DATA");
    FOR I:=1 TO N DO
      BEGIN
        READLN(A);
        S:=S+A
      END
  END;
PROCEDURE AVERAGE;
  BEGIN
    M:=S/FLOAT(N);
    WRITELN("MEAN=",M)
  END;
BEGIN %MAIN PROGRAM%
  WRITELN("INPUT SAMPLE SIZE");
  READLN(N);
  ENTER;
  AVERAGE
END.
```

The FOR I:=1 TO N DO part of the program sets a counter, I to 1 and then carries out the instructions between the BEGIN and the END which immediately follow. The counter I is then set to 2 and the instructions between the BEGIN and the END are carried out again. The process is repeated until and including the time when the counter I becomes equal to N. In program 25, the FOR loop is embedded within the Procedure ENTER. Within the FOR loop data values are input and added to the summation variable S. When all of the data have been input and summed by the Procedure ENTER, the mean is then calculated by the Procedure AVERAGE. Note that in the calculation of the mean M, FLOAT(N) is used to convert the interger N into its floating point equivalent.

In the BASIC program 26, repetition of input and summation is achieved by the FOR NEXT loop between lines 160 and 190. This loop is embedded within the subroutine ENTER. The instructions between the FOR and the NEXT are repeatedly carried out, with the counter I being incremented on each cycle of the loop until it becomes equal to N.

The reader is urged to trace the flow of control through the BASIC and the PASCAL programs given here, and to note the close similarity between the structure and the function of the programs in both languages.

BASIC

```
100 REM PROGRAM 26
110 REM AVERAGE
120 GOTO260
130 REM SUBROUTINE ENTER
140    S=0
150    PRINT"INPUT DATA"
160    FORI=1TON
170       INPUTA
180       S=S+A
190    NEXTI
200 RETURN
210 REM SUBROUTINE AVERAGE
220    M=S/N
230    PRINT"MEAN= ";M
240 RETURN
250 REM MAIN PROGRAM
260    PRINT"INPUT SAMPLE SIZE"
270    INPUTN
280    GOSUB140
290    GOSUB220
300 END
```

REPEAT UNTIL loops

In PASCAL and in some versions of BASIC it is possible to construct loops using REPEAT and UNTIL statements. The statement block between the REPEAT and the UNTIL will *always* be carried out at least once. The REPEAT causes the statement block to be performed, the UNTIL tests whether a specified condition is TRUE or FALSE, and thus whether the statement block will be repeated again. Consider the following program:

Input a number. Multiply by two and print out the answer. Repeat the multiplication process etc until the answer is greater than 100. Then print out the word FINISHED, and end the program.

PASCAL

```
%PROGRAM 27%
%REPEAT UNTIL LOOP%
VAR
   X:REAL;
BEGIN
   READLN(X);
   REPEAT
     X:=X*2.0;
     WRITELN(X);
   UNTIL X>100.0;
   WRITELN("FINISHED")
END.
```

The operations : X:=2.0; and WRITELN(X); will be repeated until the condition X>100.0 becomes TRUE.

In some versions of BASIC, REPEAT–UNTIL loops can be constructed directly as in PASCAL. This is shown in program 28.

BASIC * * *

```
100 REM PROGRAM 28
110 REM EXPLICIT REPEAT UNTIL LOOP
120 INPUTX
130 REPEAT
140   X=X*2
150   PRINTX
160 UNTILX>100
170 PRINT"FINISHED"
180 END
```

However, the words REPEAT and UNTIL are not supported by many versions of BASIC. Nevertheless, REPEAT–UNTIL loops can easily be constructed by the use of IF–THEN statements, as shown in program 29.

BASIC

```
100 REM PROGRAM 29
110 REM IMPLICIT REPEAT UNTIL LOOP
120 INPUTX
130 REM REPEAT
140   X=X*2
150   PRINTX
160 REM UNTILX>100
170 IFX<=100THEN140
180 PRINT"FINISHED"
190 END
```

It can be seen that lines 140 and 150 will be repeatedly executed until the condition X<=100 becomes FALSE (or in other words, until X>100 becomes TRUE). To demonstrate the REPEAT–UNTIL loops of programs 27-29 in action, run the program and input 50. The computer will then print out:

```
100
200
FINISHED
```

Then run the program again, and input 150. The computer will then print out:

>   300
>   FINISHED

WHILE loops

With the REPEAT—UNTIL loop structure, the condition is tested *after* the statement block has been executed. This is why the statement block will always be executed at least once.

With WHILE loops however, the condition is tested *before* the statement block is executed, so the statement block need never be executed at all. Consider the following program:

Input a number and then as long as the number is less than or equal to 100, multiply by two, and print out the answer. Repeat the multiplication etc while the answer is less than or equal to 100. Then print out the word FINISHED, and end the program.

PASCAL

```
%PROGRAM 30%
%WHILE LOOP%
VAR
   X:REAL;
BEGIN
   READLN(X);
   WHILE X<=100.0 DO
   BEGIN
      X:=X*2.0;
      WRITELN(X)
   END;
   WRITELN("FINISHED")
END.
```

If the condition X<=100.0 is TRUE then the statement block between BEGIN and END; immediately following the DO, will be executed. If the condition is FALSE, then the statement block will not be executed.

Some versions of BASIC support WHILE loops which are contained between WHILE and WEND, or WHILE AND ENDWHILE statements as shown in program 31 below.

BASIC * * *

```
100 REM PROGRAM 31
110 REM EXPLICIT WHILE LOOP
120 INPUTX
130 WHILEX<=100
140   X=X*2
150   PRINTX
160 WEND
170 PRINT"FINISHED"
180 END
```

However, many versions of BASIC do not support WHILE. Nevertheless, it is a simple matter to program WHILE loop structures by the use of IF—THEN and GOTO statements as shown in Program 32.

BASIC

```
100 REM PROGRAM 32
110 REM IMPLICIT WHILE LOOP
120 INPUTX
130 REM WHILEX<=100
140 IFX>100THEN190
150   X=X*2
160   PRINTX
170 REM WEND
180 GOTO140
190 PRINT"FINISHED"
200 END
```

To demonstrate the WHILE loops of programs 30-32, run the program and input 50. The computer will print out:

```
100
200
FINISHED
```

which is exactly what the REPEAT—UNTIL loop did. However, run the program again and input 150. The computer will print out:

```
FINISHED
```

The reader should follow the flow of control through the REPEAT—UNTIL and the WHILE loop programs in order to reinforce his/her understanding of the difference between them.

If you are using a version of BASIC which does not directly support REPEAT—UNTIL and WHILE—WEND statements, then it is good practice to use REM statements to indicate where these structures are in your programs as shown by lines 130 and 160 in program 29, and lines 130 and 170 in program 32.

ARRAYS

So far, when we have input data values for our programs to process, the values have been processed as soon as they were entered. However, often we have data in the form of lists of numbers or tables of numbers. It may be necessary to input the whole table of data before processing begins. The structures which are used to contain tables of data are called ARRAYS. ARRAYS can have a number of dimensions. A one dimensional ARRAY is like a list of data values. A two dimensional ARRAY is like a table of data values. A three dimensional ARRAY is like a book of tables, and so on. (Some language implementations set an upper limit to the number of dimensions which an ARRAY can have, and in some versions of BASIC, only one dimensional ARRAYS are allowed. (Appendix 2 shows how to create a 2 or 3 dimensional ARRAY from a one dimensional ARRAY) .)

In both PASCAL and BASIC, an ARRAY has to be declared before it can be used. The ARRAY declaration serves to dimension the ARRAY, setting aside sufficient memory space for the data which may be contained within the ARRAY. In PASCAL the ARRAY is declared along with the other variables in the VAR declaration part of the program. e.g.:

    VAR
      A:ARRAY[3,2] OF REAL

This declares an ARRAY called A which can be regarded as being a table with 3 rows and 2 columns, and which can hold real numbers. This ARRAY therefore, has 6 elements. Each element can be identified by two 'subscripts' which are contained in square brackets. Thus, A[2,2] refers to the data value in the ARRAY A which occurs in row 2, column 2, etc.

(The reader should consult Appendix 1 for the more general ARRAY declaration in PASCAL. The coding shown in the present text is specifically for SP-4015 PASCAL, however, the differences are trivial.)

In BASIC, an ARRAY is declared by means of a DIM statement. The equivalent ARRAY declaration in BASIC is given below:

    100 DIM A(3,2)

Consider the following program to input numbers into an ARRAY with 3 rows and 2 columns, row by row, and then print the numbers out in sequence, column by column.

PASCAL

```
%PROGRAM 33%
%INPUT AND OUTPUT AN ARRAY%
VAR
   I,J:INTEGER;
   A:ARRAY[3,2]OF REAL;
PROCEDURE INPUT;
   BEGIN
```

```
            FOR I:=1 TO 3 DO
               BEGIN
                  FOR J:=1 TO 2 DO
                     BEGIN
                        READLN(A[I,J])
                     END
               END
         END;
      PROCEDURE OUTPUT;
         BEGIN
            FOR I:=1 TO 2 DO
               BEGIN
                  FOR J:=1 TO 3 DO
                     BEGIN
                        WRITELN(A[J,I])
                     END
               END
         END;
      %MAIN PROGRAM%
      BEGIN
         INPUT;
         OUTPUT
      END.
```

the same program in BASIC is as follows:

BASIC

```
100 REM PROGRAM 34
110 REM INPUT AND OUTPUT AN ARRAY
120 DIMA(3,2)
130 GOTO290
140 REM SUBROUTINE INPUT
150    FORI=1TO3
160       FORJ=1TO2
170          INPUTA(I,J)
```

```
180     NEXTJ
190   NEXTI
200 RETURN
210 REM SUBROUTINE OUTPUT
220   FORI=1TO2
230     FORJ=1TO3
240       PRINTA(J,I)
250     NEXTJ
260   NEXTI
270 RETURN
280 REM MAIN PROGRAM
290   GOSUB150
300   GOSUB220
310 END
```

Run the program and input the numbers:

1 2 3 4 5 6.

In its main memory, the computer will put these numbers into a two dimensional ARRAY called A, as follows:

1 2
3 4
5 6

The computer will then print out:

1
3
5
2
4
6

DATA, READ and RESTORE statements

In BASIC it is possible to include data as part of the program. This is done by the use of DATA statements as follows:

e.g.
```
100DATA2,2.5,5,8
110DATA4,3,3.9
```

Even though we have used two lines to hold the data values, what we have really done is to create a data queue as follows:

2,2.5,5,8,4,3,3.9

We can create a data queue of any length simply by adding more DATA statements.

The data values in the data queue are accessed by means of READ statements.

Consider the following program:

BASIC

```
100 REM PROGRAM 35
110 REM READ DATA
120 READX
130 PRINTX
140 READY,Z
150 PRINTY,Z
160 END
170 DATA2.5,3,4
```

The first READ statement in the program reads the first data value from the data queue, the second READ statement reads the second, and third data values from the data queue. The computer will print out:

2.5
3   4

Each time a READ statement is met in the program, a 'pointer' moves along the data queue to indicate the next data value to be read by the next READ statement.

It is possible to restore the 'pointer' to the beginning of the data queue by means of the RESTORE statement. Thus, the program 36 below:

BASIC

```
100 REM PROGRAM 36
110 REM READ DATA RESTORE
120 READX
130 PRINTX
140 RESTORE
150 READY,Z
160 PRINTY,Z
170 END
180 DATA2.5,3,4
```

will print out:

    2.5
    2.5   3

Note that the DATA statements *can* occur *after* the END statement.

There is no similar DATA structure in PASCAL.

RECURSION

Recursion is said to occur when a sub-program calls itself. Not all language implementations allow full recursion i.e. for a routine to continue to call itself effectively without limit.

Programs 37 and 38 show a very simple example of recursion. In the PASCAL program 37 the PROCEDURE RECURSE calls itself. The result is that 1 is added to 1 and the result 2 is printed out. RECURSE is called and 2 is added to the 2 and the result is printed out, and so on.

PASCAL

```
%PROGRAM 37%
%SIMPLE RECURSION%
VAR
   X:INTEGER;
```

```
PROCEDURE RECURSE;
  BEGIN
    X:=X+1;
    WRITELN(X);
    RECURSE
  END;
%MAIN PROGRAM%
BEGIN
  X:=1;
  RECURSE
END.
```

In the BASIC program 38 the SUBROUTINE called RECURSE which starts at line 140 calls itself at line 160. The result is the same as with the PASCAL program 37. However, in SP-5025 BASIC the program does not run 'forever'.

BASIC

```
100 REM PROGRAM 38
110 REM SIMPLE RECURSION
120 GOTO190
130 REM SUBROUTINE RECURSE
140   X=X+1
150   PRINTX
160   GOSUB140
170 RETURN
180 REM MAIN PROGRAM
190   X=1
200   GOSUB140
210 END
```

The computer prints out:

    2
    3
    4
    5

6
7
8
9
10
11
12
13
14
15
16

and then terminates with an error message that a GOSUB error has occurred at line 160. This is because this particular interpreter only allows subroutines to be nested 16 deep. However, other BASIC interpreters will allow the recursive call to continue indefinitely.

Recursion can save repetitious programming but it is generally agreed that in most cases it is best avoided unless the alternative is very complex or obscure.

Structured sorting programs

The sorting programs given below incorporate all of the structures described in previous sections. Each program contains three sub-programs. One sub-program is to input the data to be sorted. A second sub-program sorts the data into numerical order, and a third sub-program prints out the sorted data. The job of the main program is to call the sub-program in the correct order.

Programs 39 and 41 show a BUBBLESORT which is one of the simplest sorting algorithms. Program 39 gives BUBBLESORT in PASCAL while program 40 gives BUBBLESORT in BASIC which explicitly supports REPEAT,WHILE and ELSE. The similarity between programs 39 and 40 is striking. Program 41 on the other hand, is written in SP5025 BASIC which does not support REPEAT,WHILE or ELSE. However, these structures have been implicitly created in the program as shown by the REM statements. Again, the similarity between programs 39 and 41 is striking.

Programs 42 to 44 show QUICKSORT which is one of the fastest known sorting algorithms. The reader is once again urged to notice the close similarity between the PASCAL and the BASIC programs.

The structure which is evident in the PASCAL programs is in fact forced into existence by the nature of the PASCAL language. However, the structure (PASCAL-like) which is evident in the BASIC programs, is due entirely to the programmer.

PASCAL

```
%PROGRAM 39%
%PROGRAM BUBBLESORT%
VAR
   LIST:ARRAY[100]OF REAL;
   N:INTEGER;
PROCEDURE INPUT;
VAR
   I:INTEGER;
BEGIN
   WRITELN("INPUT SAMPLE SIZE");
   READLN(N);
   WRITELN("ENTER DATA VALUES");
   FOR I:=1 TO N DO
      READLN(LIST[I]);
END;
PROCEDURE OUTPUT;
VAR
   I:INTEGER;
BEGIN
   WRITELN("SORTED DATA");
   FOR I:=1 TO N DO
      WRITELN(LIST[I]);
END;
PROCEDURE BUBBLESORT;
```

```
     VAR
        K,I:INTEGER;
        TEMP:REAL;
     BEGIN
        REPEAT
           K:=0;
           I:=1;
           WHILE I<N DO
              BEGIN
                 IF LIST[I]>LIST[I+1]THEN
                    BEGIN
                       TEMP:=LIST[I];
                       LIST[I]:=LIST[I+1];
                       LIST[I+1]:=TEMP;
                       K:=1;
                       I:=I+1;
                    END
                  ELSE I:=I+1;
              END;
        UNTIL K=0
     END;
     %MAIN PROGRAM%
     BEGIN
        INPUT;
        BUBBLESORT;
        OUTPUT
     END.
```

BASIC***

```
100 REM PROGRAM 40
110 REM PROGRAM BUBBLESORT
120 REM WITH EXPLICIT STRUCTURING
130 DIML(100)
140 REM TRANSFER CONTROL TO MAIN PROG.
150 GOTO450
```

```
160 REM SUBROUTINE INPUT
170   PRINT"INPUT SAMPLE SIZE"
180   INPUTN
190   PRINT"INPUT DATA"
200   FORI=1TON
210     INPUTL(I)
220   NEXTI
230 RETURN
240 REM SUBROUTINE OUTPUT
250   PRINT"SORTED DATA"
260   FORI=1TON
270     PRINTL(I)
280   NEXTI
290 RETURN
300 REM SUBROUTINE BUBBLESORT
310   REPEAT
320     C=0
330     I=1
340     WHILEI<N
350       IFL(I)>L(I+1)THEN360ELSE400
360       TE=L(I)
370       L(I)=L(I+1)
380       L(I+1)=TE
390       C=1
400       I=I+1
410     WEND
420   UNTILC=0
430 RETURN
440 REM MAIN PROGRAM
450   REM CALL SUBROUTINE INPUT
460   GOSUB170
470   REM CALL SUBROUTINE BUBBLESORT
480   GOSUB310
490   REM CALL SUBROUTINE OUTPUT
500   GOSUB250
510 END
```

BASIC

```
100 REM PROGRAM 41
110 REM PROGRAM BUBBLESORT
120 REM WITH IMPLICIT STRUCTURING
130 DIML(100)
140 REM TRANSFER CONTROL TO MAIN PROG.
150 GOTO500
160 REM SUBROUTINE INPUT
170    PRINT"INPUT SAMPLE SIZE"
180    INPUTN
190    PRINT"INPUT DATA"
200    FORI=1TON
210       INPUTL(I)
220    NEXTI
230 RETURN
240 REM SUBROUTINE OUTPUT
250    FORI=1TON
260       PRINTL(I)
270    NEXTI
280 RETURN
290 REM SUBROUTINE BUBBLESORT
300    REM REPEAT
310       C=0
320       I=1
330       REM WHILEI<N
340          IFI>=NTHEN460
350          IFL(I)>L(I+1)THEN380
360          REM ELSE
370          GOTO420
380          TE=L(I)
390          L(I)=L(I+1)
400          L(I+1)=TE
410          C=1
420          I=I+1
430       REM WEND
```

```
440     GOTO340
450   REM UNTILC=0
460    IFC<>0THEN310
470 RETURN
480 REM MAIN PROGRAM
490   REM CALL SUBROUTINE INPUT
500    GOSUB170
510    REM CALL SUBROUTINE BUBBLESORT
520    GOSUB310
530    REM CALL SUBROUTINE OUTPUT
540    GOSUB250
550 END
```

PASCAL

```
%PROGRAM 42%
%PROGRAM QUICKSORT%
VAR
   LIST:ARRAY[100]OF REAL;
   N:INTEGER;
PROCEDURE INPUT;
VAR
   I:INTEGER;
BEGIN
   WRITELN("INPUT SAMPLE SIZE");
   READLN(N);
   WRITELN("ENTER DATA VALUES");
   FOR I:=1 TO N DO
      READLN(LIST[I]);
END;
PROCEDURE OUTPUT;
VAR
   I:INTEGER;
BEGIN
   WRITELN("SORTED DATA");
```

```
    FOR I:=1 TO N DO
       WRITELN(LIST[I]);
END;
PROCEDURE QUICKSORT;
VAR
  FIRST,LAST,J,I,TOP:INTEGER;
  DLINE,TEMP:REAL;
  STACK:ARRAY[25]OF INTEGER;
BEGIN
  STACK[1]:=1;
  STACK[2]:=N;
  TOP:=2;
  REPEAT
    LAST:=STACK[TOP];
    TOP:=TOP-1;
    FIRST:=STACK[TOP];
    TOP:=TOP-1;
    I:=FIRST;
    REPEAT
      J:=LAST;
      DLINE:=LIST[(FIRST+LAST)DIV 2];
      REPEAT
        WHILE LIST[I]<DLINE DO
           I:=I+1;
        WHILE LIST[J]>DLINE DO
           J:=J-1;
        IF I<=J THEN
           BEGIN
             TEMP:=LIST[I];
             LIST[I]:=LIST[J];
             LIST[J]:=TEMP;
             I:=I+1;
             J:=J-1;
           END
      UNTIL I>J;
```

```
            IF FIRST<J THEN
               BEGIN
                  TOP:=TOP+1;
                  STACK[TOP]:=FIRST;
                  TOP:=TOP+1;
                  STACK[TOP]:=J;
               END;
            FIRST:=I
         UNTIL FIRST>=LAST
      UNTIL TOP=0
   END;
   %MAIN PROGRAM%
   BEGIN
      INPUT;
      QUICKSORT;
      OUTPUT;
   END.
```

BASIC * * *

```
100 REM PROGRAM 43
110 REM PROGRAM QUICKSORT
120 REM WITH EXPLICIT STRUCTURING
130 DIML(100)
140 REM TRANSFER CONTROL TO MAIN PROG.
150 GOTO690
160 REM SUBROUTINE INPUT
170    PRINT"INPUT SAMPLE SIZE"
180    INPUTN
190    PRINT"INPUT DATA"
200    FORI=1TON
210       INPUTL(I)
220    NEXTI
230 RETURN
240 REM SUBROUTINE OUTPUT
250    PRINT"SORTED DATA"
```

```
260     FORI=1TON
270       PRINTL(I)
280     NEXTI
290   RETURN
300 REM SUBROUTINE QUICKSORT
310     DIMS(25)
320     S(1)=1
330     S(2)=N
340     T=2
350     REPEAT
360       LA=S(T)
370       T=T-1
380       FI=S(T)
390       T=T-1
400       I=FI
410       REPEAT
420         J=LA
430         DL=L((FI+LA)/2)
440         REPEAT
450           WHILEL(I)<DL
460             I=I+1
470           WEND
480           WHILEL(J)>DL
490             J=J-1
500           WEND
510           IFI<=JTHEN520ELSE570
520           TE=L(I)
530           L(I)=L(J)
540           L(J)=TE
550           I=I+1
560           J=J-1
570         UNTILI>J
580         IFFI<JTHEN590ELSE630
590         T=T+1
600         S(T)=FI
```

```
610         T=T+1
620         S(T)=J
630         FI=I
640       UNTILFI>=LA
650   UNTILT=0
660 RETURN
670 REM MAIN PROGRAM
680   REM CALL SUBROUTINE INPUT
690   GOSUB170
700   REM CALL SUBROUTINE QUICKSORT
710   GOSUB310
720   REM CALL SUBROUTINE OUTPUT
730   GOSUB250
740 END
```

BASIC

```
100 REM PROGRAM 44
110 REM PROGRAM QUICKSORT
120 REM WITH IMPLICIT STRUCTURING
130 DIML(100)
140 REM TRANSFER CONTROL TO MAIN PROG.
150 GOTO800
160 REM INPUT ROUTINE
170   PRINT"INPUT SAMPLE SIZE"
180   INPUTN
190   PRINT"INPUT DATA"
200   FORI=1TON
210     INPUTL(I)
220   NEXTI
230 RETURN
240 REM SUBROUTINE OUTPUT
250   PRINT"SORTED DATA"
260   FORI=1TON
270     PRINTL(I)
280   NEXTI
```

```
290 RETURN
300 REM SUBROUTINE QUICKSORT
310   DIMS(25)
320   S(1)=1
330   S(2)=N
340   T=2
350   REM REPEAT
360     LA=S(T)
370     T=T-1
380     FI=S(T)
390     T=T-1
400     I=FI
410     REM REPEAT
420       J=LA
430       DL=L((FI+LA)/2)
440       REM REPEAT
450         REM WHILEL(I)<DL
460           IFL(I)>=DLTHEN510
470           I=I+1
480         REM WEND
490         GOTO460
500         REM WHILEL(J)>DL
510           IFL(J)<=DLTHEN550
520           J=J-1
530         REM WEND
540         GOTO510
550         IFI<=JTHEN580
560         REM ELSE
570         GOTO640
580         TE=L(I)
590         L(I)=L(J)
600         L(J)=TE
610         I=I+1
620         J=J-1
630       REM UNTILI>J
```

```
640        IFI<=JTHEN440
650        IFFI<JTHEN680
660        REM ELSE
670        GOTO720
680        T=T+1
690        S(T)=FI
700        T=T+1
710        S(T)=J
720        FI=I
730      REM UNTILFI>=LA
740      IFFI<LATHEN410
750    REM UNTILT=0
760    IFT<>0THEN350
770 RETURN
780 REM MAIN PROGRAM
790    REM CALL SUBROUTINE INPUT
800    GOSUB170
810    REM CALL SUBROUTINE QUICKSORT
820    GOSUB310
830    REM CALL SUBROUTINE OUTPUT
840    GOSUB250
850 END
```

As they are, programs 43 and 44 work fine. However, if we replace the END statements with GOTO690 in program 43, and GOTO800 in program 44, the effect is to be able to input one set of numbers after another, and each set will be sorted. The program can only be stopped by breaking in. If we try to run the modified program however, it will work fine for the first set of data but will then give an error message when we enter the second set of data. This is because at line 310 the program tries to declare the ARRAY S. However, this ARRAY was declared the first time that the SUBROUTINE QUICKSORT was called. A given array can only be declared once. The solution is simple: just take the declaration of ARRAY S out of the SUBROUTINE QUICKSORT and place it on line 130 or somewhere else. e.g.:

130 DIM L(100),S(25)

We have seen that even when the control structures BEGIN—END ; IF—THEN—ELSE ; REPEAT—UNTIL ; and WHILE—WEND are not explicitly supported by a particular language implementation, it is possible to construct them by using statements which *are* present in the language. Thus, the systematic programming process called structured programming, which makes use of these control structures, and modular program design, are quite possible even with an unstructured implementation of BASIC.

It was stated at the beginning of this book that the aim of the book is not to cover in depth all of the features of BASIC and PASCAL. In fact we have concentrated on the common ground between the two languages. PASCAL however, has data structures which make it a very powerful language. These are beyond the scope of this text, because in this area there is little common ground between BASIC and PASCAL. If the reader has become interested in PASCAL programming, he/she should study data structures from an advanced text on PASCAL.

Finally, it should be noted that in most books the word Pascal is not written in capitals as it is in this book. This is because Pascal is not an acronym but a person's name. I have departed from this tradition simply for personal preference.

APPENDIX 1

Standard PASCAL

PROGRAM

Standard PASCAL requires that the program starts with the word PROGRAM. The word PROGRAM is then followed by the name of the program, and then, in brackets, the word OUTPUT, or the words INPUT,OUTPUT. e.g.:

    PROGRAM AVERAGE (INPUT,OUTPUT);

This states that the program is called AVERAGE, and that information is both input to and output from the program. However, PROGRAM DISPLAY (OUTPUT); states that the program is called DISPLAY and that it only outputs information but does not require any information to be input.

Writing strings

In standard PASCAL, single quotation marks are used inside brackets to delimit strings, e.g.:

    WRITELN('STRING');

Comments

In standard PASCAL, comments are usually enclosed in braces {COMMENT}. However, many computers do not have braces in their character sets so various PASCAL implementations use other symbols such as the % symbol %, or sometimes (*COMMENT*).

ARRAY declaration

In standard PASCAL, an ARRAY having 3 rows and 2 columns, containing real numbers, and being called A would be declared as follows:

    VAR
        A:ARRAY[1..3,1..2] OF REAL;

In standard PASCAL we are able to specify the range of the 'subscripts' for the rows and columns etc. In the example above, we have specified that the row 'subscripts' range from 1 to 3, and that the column 'subscripts' range from 1 to 2. That is, we have declared a 3 by 2 ARRAY. However, we could have declared our ARRAY as follows for example:

    VAR
        A:ARRAY [6..8,4..5] OF REAL;

This would also be a 3 by 2 ARRAY but with a different range of 'subscripts'.

TYPE declaration

In standard PASCAL it is possible to declare data to be of particular defined TYPEs. For example, suppose that in a particular program you were wanting to declare a large number of two dimensional ARRAYs which could hold real numbers, it could be done as follows:

```
TYPE
    MATRIX = ARRAY [1..2, 1..2] OF REAL;
VAR
    A,B,C,D,E,F: MATRIX;
```

This will clearly save time if variables of TYPE MATRIX need to be declared in various parts of the program.

APPENDIX 2

Creating 2 or 3 dimensional ARRAYS from a 1 dimensional ARRAY

To declare a 2 dimensional ARRAY with R rows and C columns, the equivalent of the BASIC:

DIM A(R,C)   is:
DIM A(R*C)

To index an element in the ARRAY A as A(I,J), we use:

A(C*(I−1)+J).

To declare a 3 dimensional ARRAY with R rows, C columns, and L layers, the equivalent of the BASIC:

DIM A(R,C,L)   is:
DIM A(R*C*L) .

To index an element in the ARRAY A as A(I,J,K), we use:

A(C*(I−1)+J+R*C*(K−1))

By this means it is possible to eliminate the possible disadvantages of a language implementation that only supports 1 dimensional ARRAYS.